by Bonita Ferraro

Editorial Offices: Glenview, Illinois • Parsippany, New Jersey • New York, New York
Sales Offices: Needham, Massachusetts • Duluth, Georgia • Glenview, Illinois
Coppell, Texas • Ontario, California • Mesa, Arizona

ISBN: 0-328-13283-7

A mother frog lays her eggs in the pond. She kicks her powerful back legs and leaps away. Soon something wonderful will happen.

The tiny frog eggs have no shell. They are covered with clear jelly. The frog eggs stick together in big clumps.

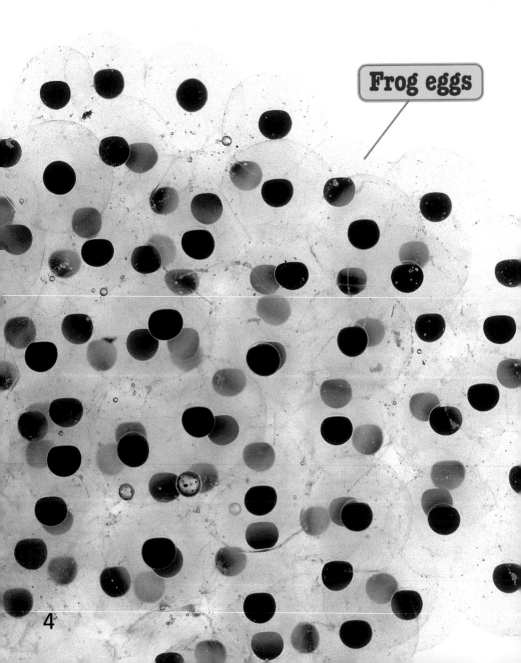

Frog eggs

Inside each egg is the beginning of a frog. The black dot is a tadpole growing. The tadpoles change as they grow. Something wonderful begins to happen.

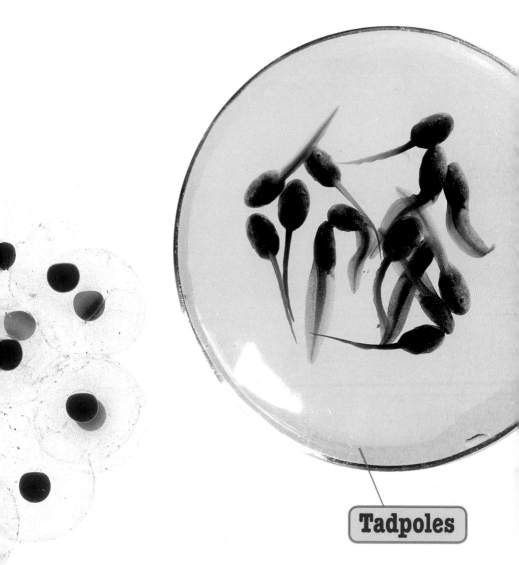

Tadpoles

The new tadpoles hatch from their eggs. They look like little fish. The tadpoles have gills like fish to help them breathe under water. The tadpoles eat tiny water plants.

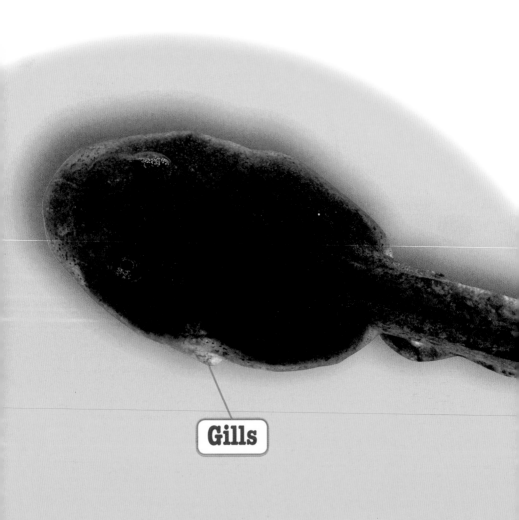

Gills

Now hind legs grow. After a while the tadpole grows lungs. Lungs let the tadpole breathe air too. Something wonderful is happening.

Hind legs

Now the tadpole changes again.
Front legs come out, one at a time. Its
eyes grow larger. Its mouth grows wider.
Now it looks like a frog with a tail.

Front legs

The tadpole's tail goes away. Then it crawls out of the water. The tadpole is a froglet. The froglet has shed its tadpole skin. Something wonderful has happened.

Froglet

The tadpole has become a frog. It can live on land or in the water. The frog uses its long, sticky tongue to eat insects.

One day the frog will lay eggs in the pond. Inside each egg a tadpole will change and grow. Something wonderful will happen all over again.

Frog

Sticky tongue

Follow the diagram. The frog lays the eggs. What happens next? What happens last?